Chameleon and other poems

life poems from the 20ᵗʰ Century

BY BEST SELLING AUTHOR
OLUSOLA SOPHIA ANYANWU

Copyright © Sophia Anyanwu 2020

The right of Sophia Anyanwu to be identified as author of this work has been asserted by her in accordance with the Copyright, Designs and Patents Act 1988.

All rights reserved.

No part of this publication may be reproduced or transmitted in any form or by any means, electronic or mechanical, including photocopy, recording, or any information storage and retrieval system, without permission in writing from the publisher.

Cover design by Liz Carter

ISBN 978-1-915398-07-9

4/5 STAR REVIEWS

Heartfelt writing. An understandable and relatable collection of poems. **C Davis**

Written from the heart. The prolific author Sophia Anyanwu has presented her readers with a daring collection of word pictures that push out boundaries and challenge expectations. I found IT partially interesting. This is not a collection of quaint, rhyming poems. Her heartfelt lines of prose have a distinctive beat that resonate like notes from an African drum. Fond of repetition, for she writes in Nigerian English, Sophia examines issues from many different angles: do read A LIFE PROTEST. There is a taste within it for us all. I was given a review copy of this book, but my views are my own. **Sophie Neville**

Inspiring poems. Enjoyed reading this collection of poems. Very inspiring read. Love the spiritual element of it. **Modupe Peters**

Other books by Olusola Sophia Anyanwu

Stories for Younger Generations
Tales for Younger Generations
Sophia's Fables for Younger Generations
Stories for Older Generations
The Captive's Crown
Turning the Clock Hands Backwards or Anthem
The Confession
The Crown
Their Journey
The Robe

www.olusolasophiaanyanwuauthor.com

THIS WORK IS DEDICATED TO THE AUTHOR
AND FINISHER OF MY FAITH.

Contents

1 ~ A LAMENTATION	1
2 ~ FUTILE EFFORTS	2
3 ~ WITH NO EXCEPTION	3
4 ~ LIFE PROTEST	5
5 ~ AN ALTERNATIVE	15
6 ~ COSMIC PLEA	18
7 ~ THE LOVING FATHER	20
8 ~ WHERE IS GOD?	22
9 ~ FATHER	27
10 ~ MOTHER	29
11 ~ BABY SISTER	31
12 ~ THE NEW ARRIVAL	32
13 ~ MIDDLE SISTER	33
14 ~ YOUNGEST BROTHER	34
15 ~ YOUNGER BROTHER	35
16 ~ TRANSITION	36
17 ~ ON TRANSITION	37
18 ~ OUR FATHER	38
19 ~ THE EXPECTED CHILD	39

20 ~ THE CALL	40
21 ~ THE UNCONTROLLABLE DRUM	41
22 ~ THE WEAKER FORM	42
23 ~ SHE	43
24 ~ THE POOR CHILD	44
25 ~ THE SUSPENDED PARCEL	45
26 ~ SHAPED EIGHT DRUMS	47
27 ~ LURED	48
28 ~ IT	49
29 ~ VICTIM	50
30 ~ CHAMELEON	51
31 ~ THE ADHESIVE FIGHT	53
32 ~ CONFLICT	54
33 ~ HATCHING	55
34 ~ TEMPTATION CONQUERED	57
35 ~ THE MAIDEN'S PLEA	58
36 ~ REGRET	59
37 ~ OPPORTUNITY KNOCKS ONCE	60
38 ~ "THEY"	61
39 ~ MEMOIR FOR A LOVED PET	62
40 ~ THE INSPIRING CALL	69

41 ~ SOURCE	71
42 ~ REVERBERATING FORM	73
43 ~ THURSDAY'S DAWN CHILD	74
44 ~ THE SELECTION	75
45 ~ NON-IDENTICAL TWINS	76
46 ~ LADY EYE	77
47 ~ 'LA BOUCHE'	78
48 ~ ORIGINAL ROOTS	80
49 ~ INTEGRATION OPTED	81
50 ~ CONQUERED?	82
51 ~ BLISSFUL 'PRISON'	84
52 ~ POOR MOTHER	86
53 ~ ONE THEN TWO	88
54 ~ AFRICA	89
55 ~ PIANO	90
56 ~ THE FEET	91
57 ~ ORIENTATION	93
58 ~ THE WHITE OVER BLACK MAN	95
59 ~ THE UNTRODDEN FIELD	97
60 ~ EARTH AND PARADISE	98
61 ~ THE PRIVATE STREAM	100

62 ~ THE SPIRIT AND THE FLOW	101
63 ~ THE THREE PRISONS	102
64 ~ THE NOVICE	103
65 ~ TWO MARKS	104
66 ~ EBBING TIDE	105
67 ~ THE CIRCLE OF GREEN	106
68 ~ J.J.C	107
69 ~ FATE	108
70 ~ FREEDOM [AFTER AN EXAM]	109
71 ~ THE CYKL	111
72 ~ DO YOU KNOW?	112
73 ~ THE PLACE OF ART	113
About the Poet	115

Protests and Futility

1 ~ A LAMENTATION

Alas!!
I that I was is no more
I am now what I am not
I to be what I was
Can never be me no more
Going nearer home
Is further alienation
I am at now a 2-way image!!

2 ~ FUTILE EFFORTS

We were stuffed
With the paper and the word,
For future ambitions and aspirations,
With tremendous efforts
We coped through,
Only to receive a future
Of despair and frustration.

3 ~ WITH NO EXCEPTION

Everybody said the same thing,
That the world was 'hard',
Thinking critically wise
Saw the fact as an assumption,
Thus the possibility of an exception—

Somewhere, the world must be 'soft',
As a human being, I found the human world too hard,
Going to the animal kingdom
It was worse,
In the sea world
It was no better,
And into the plant kingdom
It was grim,

In the spirit world
It was no better,

Going to the space world
It was worse,

In desperation I remembered Heaven,
There, I had to appeal to be returned,
Earth to be who I am meant to be!

4 ~ LIFE PROTEST

A melancholy verse

Woe betide me!
That I was born
What for?
To be a living disgrace
A living let down
A frustrating existence,
Today, April 20th 1980;
I do not know whether
I should curse the day
I was born.

I feel dejected
I feel exasperated
Frustrated and disappointed
Depressed, unhappy
Fed up with myself,

With the world and life
I am a washout in academics,
I fail to understand, grasp, and remember
Always confused and chaotic,
When failure surfaces,
It must be me!

I'm a wretch even socially,
My existence embarrasses me,
I feel and suffer from inferiority complex
But why me?
Don't ask me a dunce
You think 'I know why!?'
I'm incomparable
Any day and anywhere
I do not maintain a stable
Standard and profile
I feel disgusted with myself.

Physically, I'm an ugly toad
Always an eyesore
Always cracking the mirrors
Nauseating blisters bulge out from my face
A set of sick pale seeds,
Arranging themselves in a mocking fashion
In my mouth, as my breath repulses others
I'm never found pleasing
My eyes were a lifeless pair

It mirrors me as a moron;
My lips, bulgy and upturned
Cannot maintain my saliva
My pods point at my crooked toes
My samba, a non-vibrating instrument
Cannot make me even sit comfortably
I'm a frigid one!
Very unsuitable
For any son of Adam,
Domestically I'm hopeless
I can't even mother for my own self.

Why is it that I should be?
Lazy for my own self?
Is it not that my own spirit,
Even despises me?
Many times I hunger and thirst
But I do nothing for myself,
My cooking is poisoning
Alas! My unwillingness to feed myself,
Even my family see me as a source of embarrassment,
A stumbling block to the family's dignity and pride,
At home, I'm a stone amongst worthy pearls
Spiritually, I've backslidden,
God ignores me all day,
Otherwise, why should I
Be hailed with miseries
Problems and misfortunes?

Why should I be lazy?
Weak, not sensual, and foolish
Ungifted, left out, and abandoned;
Yes, my body is weak!

But why shouldn't my spirit?
Be strong? No, it is weak too.
I do not pray nor go to church
Do I ever think of God?
Why should I? He ignores me!
Jesus, damn me!!
My faith is not spiritual
Rather it is conceived as fate,
Predetermined sequences of actions and events;
God, you see, I don't blame you
Not even in the least bit.

Life-wise, I'm a wreck;
I distract friends
I attract risky rumours,
I attract dangerous comrades and friends
My name is dragged in the mud,
Unlucky men meet me,
I'm never given my sincere heart's desire,
Wishes and dreams,
I'm always late informed
About things, even though important,
Confusion and shame

Disgrace and bad luck
Seem to be my companions
My fate has not been attractive;
I'm alienated from my tribe's people,
By my handicapped language ability
I'm left out from custom,
And the joys of togetherness;
The feelings of belonging
Pride and unity;
I'm a half child
Torn in-between these things;
In-between two incomplete cultures and customs

Economically I'm nought
I'm always being cheated
By cunning, clever, and wiser ones
Who doesn't love me;
I save for others and spend for others
I save for nothing,
I save not for the benefit of myself
In the least bit
Personally I don't know,
Why I'm born to this earth,
I do not know for which purpose I exist;
I have no life goals
No life ambition
No future aspirations;
I just live to please the world,

To be cheated and to cheat too,
If ever possible;
I'm always unhappy
Never having the type of friendship I crave for,
The wrong type of friends befriend me always;
I've never experienced true love and sweet companionship,
I'm easily despised
I always feel lazy
And reluctant to keep myself in existence;
I am conscious of all
That is good in life,
And of what will be good to me?
Then why don't I strive?

My body is weak
And so is my spirit,
Even within me is a sown division and hatred.
How do I help myself out?
Do I appeal to God?

God, have I been rude?
I'm too sorry!
Please forgive me for being an ingrate!
Selfish, greedy, and unreasonable I am
Foolish and very inconsiderate child
You are my Father!
You know what's best for me;
I'm not your only child

Why should I crave to seek and take all the best?
I'm very sorry
Forgive me thy foolish child!
I have refused to take all the good things
You set in this world
All within my reach and capacity;
I have refused to be matured
To desist from spoon-feeding
I have refused to be very grateful
For my own share of your blessings
Showered and endowed on me.

But my Father I protest one thing
And only one,
I feel my spirit is weak
Seriously I feel so;
Otherwise, why do I not,
Strive to accomplish all my inspirations?
Aspirations to be
More ambitious
To be a poet;
A writer;
A musician;
A faithful servant;
To be more spiritually conscious and energetic
A grateful one,
Show vitality in all I do.
Instead, to my opposing wish,

I sleep off my time and life
I'm easily contented
With the lowest and worst things
Easily contented for all
That is easily obtained
I strive for the lowest rung of the ladder;
I don't strive for what is best, only good
Why can't I strive for even better
If not the best?
Why should I always be content with the least?

I'm a very conscious being
My mind, my heart
My wishes, my dreams
My yearnings and desires
Are not in agreement;
It is my weak spirit
That forces them to accept the least
So help me God,
For a stronger spirit…
Amen.

Religion and Deities

5 ~ AN ALTERNATIVE

Ye!!!
What is it?
Ooh No!
I say, what is it?
A discovery!!
About what?
My confusion –
It has led me to discover
That I'm in the wrong place.

I can't cope
In this world,
A world of sin

Of cheating and robbery
Of lust and ingrates,
Of monsters and unreasoning
Of discrimination and selfishness
Of treachery and duplicity

Help me and deliver me!
Help me to continue;
It is much more than all these.
I'm horrified about the truth,
Of this discovery,
That I exist in such a world.
Or is it a world of mortality

Yay!!
What is it?
This discovery
About what?
No!! It can't be!!
You know, my illustrious Father,
He made two worlds
One mortal and immortal
That is discrimination!!
My Father should come here to govern
So that justice will reign supreme
Or if not otherwise
Shouldn't the good ones be transferred or left,
To dwell with my Father?

My Father,
I'm in the wrong place
I'm good and I've obeyed all your commands;
I've been waiting…
When will you come for us?

People are mocking me,
I am a stranger here,
Their ways are strange
They seem to dwell and
Accept their shameful ways

Oh Lord!
On thee I wait
Send my own guardian Angel to me,
I am lost; I am still,
Searching for your own immortal world
Is it you that can't hear me
From this mortal world
Through your pure ears?
Oh Lord, show me the map in my dream,
For I'm coming home to thee,
Thee at home.

6 ~ COSMIC PLEA

Order!
Silence!
Welcome from your different sojourns
I wish you wisdom
Dilemma!
Conflict!

This calls us all to the controversial issue
I hope you all resolve all discrepancies
Ignoring
Unyielding
This has been our attitude towards the Earth

Do we continue this way?
Desecrated!
Disobedience!
This is the attitude of the Earth

How can we pure illustrious ones contact them?
The exceptions!
The minority!
These are the few pure remnants
Perhaps they can be the representatives…

7 ~ THE LOVING FATHER

Seeing through the unbeliever's view

The Almighty, all Glorious, Ever living
Ever forgiving and illustrious Father
Sat on Heaven's highest mountain
Observing the earth as a drama.

He saw the rich man waste
Money and food,
The poor man was hungry
The good was executed,
The bad triumphed
Luck and goodwill befell the dishonest,
Honest men met ill fates
The unfaithful enjoyed benefits of the faithful
The evil ones seemed to be in favour with life

The lazy ones were given merits
As they reap the harvest and labour of the industrious,

Meanwhile,
Letters and messages in the form
Of rituals, sacrifices, prayers,
Protests and epistles
Carrying pathetic notes,
Delivered on Heaven's door.
The Almighty One looked at them all
with a sigh,
And continued watching…

8 ~ WHERE IS GOD?

Unbeliever's view

A frustrated person,
Seeking God physically
Came to me with her quest,
My solution to the true whereabouts of God,
I told her she needed to be dead;
She said her quest was already known by God,
To whom all things were possible;
So with her life she would seek God physically,
The Bible as a map had not helped,
The spirit in prayer was not strong enough,
Churchgoing had proved futile,
Reincarnation had found Earth
The only source of existence;
Fasting weakened her strength to bid her quest,
Sacred groves mocked her lonely presence.
Rituals and sacrifices had proved abortive.

Asked why her quest to see God,
Answer was that those who seek find,
Asked if she had tried native priests
through traditional means
To which she said she placed no faith;
Told her she was assuming
Discriminative and showing superiority,
As such, she was not qualified to see God physically.

She needed to go through this process,
As a prerequisite
She said it was impossible.
Reminded her that with God,
All things are possible;
She needed to know
There was only one God,
Getting through Lord Jesus to Him.
There were so many ways
To get God's attention:
Fasting, praise, and prayer
She had to find which suits her.

Family and Humanity

9 ~ FATHER

FARMER,
You have deposited your seeds.
May you reap what you sow.

You have been embraced with
Intellect, wisdom, and art.
May they give you peace of heart.
To your legal seedlings,
You have done your duty.

May they honour you in return.

Farmer
With many farms and seeds,
May you never be confused and alienated.

Regret shall not be your lot.
May life continue to shower,
Her mercies and blessings on you.

Finally lead you in peace at the end.

10~ MOTHER

Mother of five
Wife to our father
Our source of existence
That channelled five seedlings
Through a pure gate
Our greatest gift
Your five gifts are to you
Your existence and treasure

May you find in them
All that would please you,
All that would gladden you;

May you find in their existence
A pride to you;

May you find your existence
Worthy of living through them.

May they be to you
Your stored-up treasures that will
Multiply your pride and blood.
May the mouths you fed never bite you.

11 ~ BABY SISTER

You are given to us to end
What was begun;
Fifth out of five and
Third out of three
Partner to the second
In likeness to the fourth and third.
Like first, the fifth and the end.

You are also given to us,
Remain with us a symbolical treasure
And make the circle seven complete
May your circle embrace the best and never break.
You are the greatest and a treasure forever!

12 ~ THE NEW ARRIVAL

They were waiting
But on duty;
He was waiting
In anxiety and expectation;
I was waiting
But in fear, hope, pain, and joy.

At last,
The new arrival came
Bringing for me
My fear and pain only.
Life had come in the opposite direction.

13 ~ MIDDLE SISTER

Not for the need of silver and gold
Were you sent;
Nor to be an addition and make excess.
You are our pet,
More precious than silver and gold.
More to us
Than what is excess to others.

In you lies all that is precious and desired
All that is needed;
With you we shall thirst and want no more.
May your fountain remain continuous.

14 ~ YOUNGEST BROTHER

If nothing else is in our possession,
But the 'Giver',
Then we possess everything else.
If this is all we are to have
Then we want nothing else more.
If you are to represent our 'Giver',
We are satisfied, for we have all.
You're our treasured second of only two
Shall fulfil your duties and not let us down.

15 ~ YOUNGER BROTHER

A seedling turning into a tree
For a specific marked height.
Not all trees will be the same
Some will overshadow others.

So shall you sapling grow
To a mighty tree,
Shading your source from foes;
You were raised high
To be a good example to the younger ones.
You are a granted request,
To heighten low spirits
And elevate the wounded pride.

16 ~ TRANSITION

Soon I was changed…
Hairs grew longer on my body!
Visible big pores soon bulged out!
My pods developed taut buttons!
My melon seeds started singing!
My form started wavering!
My form looked like an ape on sit!
My eyes looked glassy!
My skin paled up!
Then soon, I was changed…
In the opposite direction!!

17 ~ ON TRANSITION

I was dead
but alive.

In my death,
I journeyed to life
and saw the dead;
they beckoned to me
to have their life, but
I wanted my life
though dead;
they insisted persistently
and in the struggle,
I became alive
but dead.

18 ~ OUR FATHER

Like us the children,
Our father behaves similarly
He lets us know
When distress oppresses him
Right now,
We know he is weeping
For his tears are shed
On our bosoms

19 ~ THE EXPECTED CHILD

It was with great expectations
We expected this child
Our mother had been due
Long before the delivery time
When this child came
We expected therefore,
For the child to be matured
And not a premature
But the latter was the case
The child had an alien nature
By still following alien ways
Rather than the mother's
As the child matured
It neglected those roles
And functions that were assigned to it
It was with great disappointment
We felt for this child…

20 ~ THE CALL

I got the call now;
It was a message—
The wind, my bearer
And I the receiver;
I got it while in solitude,
My spirit awakens;
The wind, mingling with the music
Vibrating in it,
Pitched louder, the sound waves;
My heart caught first
The pathos of the atmosphere.
My senses livened and
I got the call;
It was a message—
Heart rendering and pathetic
From my black brother,
That a slave he now was
Suffering, hungry, and dying…

21 ~ THE UNCONTROLLABLE DRUM

I was born with my drum
I alone hear the rhythm of my drum
No one can feel and dance to
The beats of my drum
My drum beats fastest
When the tide has cause to rise
It also refuses to beat
When the tide has cause to cease
I have no control over my drum
The tempo of my drum
Is not always my design or wish
I am no more when the beats cease.

22 ~ THE WEAKER FORM

Frail
Fragile
Delicate
Yet quite industrious
Quite laborious
Quite strong
And quite firm.
One in many
Many in one.
For a few
For a multitude
For the world.

23 ~ SHE

How beautiful she is
A black beauty she is
Nicely shaped she is
She is really what she is

Many suitors she invited to herself
Many raiders and invaders she got herself
Into trouble she got herself
She really deserves what she got herself

Too warm she was
Too inviting she was
A harlot she was
A concubine to many she was

Many and dispersed her seeds are
Full, half-blooded her seeds are
Incompatible and disagreeable her seeds are
Hateful and spiteful her once admirers are
Ever still yourself
Where is your self-pride?

24 ~ THE POOR CHILD

There he sat
Alone and abandoned
Looking wretched
Miserable and hungry
His large dead eyes
Sat without life
Looking imploringly
His heart knew
No love safe
Brutality and cruelty

He did not need pity
He did not want alms
He craved not for care
But all he longed for
Was to be owned
To have an identity
To see life positively
And experience happiness

25 ~ THE SUSPENDED PARCEL

Given a parcel in a bag
Her joy knew no bounds
Neither could it be contained

Realising with shock
The inability of knowing the contents
For a certain length of time

Anxiety and excitement embraced her
Worry and impatience as visitors
Came to reside with her;
The bag became heavier,
And she alone carried it,

But the contents she would share
The contents being very precious

Delicate and valuable they were,
Carefully carried,
Time arrived to open the parcel,
And it was not easy,
With great pain and tremendous effort,
The bag was burst open
And out came a life born
But still.

26 ~ SHAPED EIGHT DRUMS

African Rubber skinned drums
Of all sizes, but shaped eight
Automatically plays itself
By vibrating;

The rhythmic beats
Rise and fall.
It is charmed with magic:
It could turn sane insane,
It could turn into a gate,
It could carry any weight,
It could lessen people's gait.

The skirts, the owners,
The trousers, the dancers.
It is played sensuously
And danced with desire.

27 ~ LURED

First,
The eyes were appealed
The senses were in agreement
It soothed the tongues taste
The fingers itched
The feet were on and ready
The mind kept pestering and tempting
The heart needed its desires filled
Then,
The sin was carried out…

28 ~ IT

It is not a commensalism association
It is a symbiotic one.
It is not parasitic
Neither is it cupboard in nature.
It has no seasons of change
It is constant.
It is the undying flame in winter,
It is the burning passion in autumn,
It is the exchange of responses in spring.
It is the strongest force,
Invisible.

29 ~ VICTIM

At a glance
Ravenously appetising,
Weakening the powerful,
Strengthening the desire,
Heating the cold,
Stiffening the crumpled,
Making alive the dead
Is that which victimises
The weak flesh.

30 ~ CHAMELEON

You say you love me,
But it is because you desire my woman
Is that not deceit?

You say you find me beautiful,
But it is because you wish me to respond to flattery
Is that not blackmail?

You say I should go under lock and key with you,
But it is because you want to ravish my woman
Is that not treachery?

You show me your stores of wealth,
But that is because you think I will follow you
Is that not foolishness?

You shower me with material gains,
But it is because you think I will melt

Is that wisdom?
You show me your true heart,
But it is because you think I am not cheap
Is that not conviction?

You now court me faithfully and sincerely,
But it is because you want to marry me
Is it that you would not change?

31 ~ THE ADHESIVE FIGHT

Physical duel between strong and weak forms
Involving mutual agreement
The strong form masculine
The weak form feminine

At climax's peak
Both forms are

Exhausted but satisfied
Divided but in one
Separated but joined

Having fought as two
To become three or more.

32 ~ CONFLICT

You were a Romeo
And
I, not a Juliet
Sincere, hopeful and blue
Your passions were for me
Even though taken
For granted, unserious
And treated as dust by me.

Now,
You are not Romeo.
But
I am Juliet…

33 ~ HATCHING

Towards the journey's end
We met
I was alone
And thought so of you
Declining from this thought

You said we should pair up
The journey almost ended
You being a stranger and
Your ways alien to mine
I declined from pairing up

Then with you
The journey appeared longer
You became familiar with my ways
You integrated my ways
And said we should pair up
But knowing Adams

To be deceptive and insincere
Not fearing God and heartless
I declined from pairing up

But through you
I saw sincerity and honesty
The fear of God and devotion
And so became positive
Towards your intentions.

34 ~ TEMPTATION CONQUERED

Two of us alone
Together sitting
In isolation
Was like us being
The only two in the world
It was like being in Eden
Smelling the forbidden fruit
My feelings warmed towards you
You were like a magnet
Appealing and attracting
My already hot desires
Your warmth and presence
Sent me on the danger zone
You looked at me and
I felt like falling…
Suddenly,
I saw the Lucifer in you
And recoiled from the sweet danger…
Had I the power to release the freedom,
Of the forbidden fruit
I would…

35 ~ THE MAIDEN'S PLEA

For too long
A maiden I have remained
A woman I crave to be

To know the unknown
Feel the unfelt
Sense sensation
Taste the forbidden
Be wiser from the secret
Cry from the pleasurable pain
Cry for a permanent loss
Of a chaste gate that
Would be broken to let in
The womaniser

36 ~ REGRET

Cross-legged on a sofa
Looking across empty space
My thoughts fill my mind
All about you.

Sadly I remember
Our past in the past
And at present
We have nothing to offer
Except regret for the future
That would be barren
Of a past of its own.

37 ~ OPPORTUNITY KNOCKS ONCE

I was arrogant
When you in humility
Surrendered yourself and love
I trod on you and
Flung back your love and
You learnt arrogance

Looking aback
I became sober
I saw not a humble one, but
An arrogant you
Flickering hatred
In vengeance.

38 ~ "THEY"

dead to the world
but Alive to me.
nought to others
but
symbolical to me.
viewed as playthings
to be discarded
but
with me, they remain
An Everlasting Treasure.

39 ~ MEMOIR FOR A LOVED PET

December 25, 1981, 9.30am

Teddy Boy!!!
Teddy Boy!! Teddy Boy!

Where are your pets?
I've returned
Home for Xmas.
They say you are gone.
Gone for good.
To a home
I'll never see you.
Adieu, my beloved pet
Teddy Boy.

I can't believe
I'll see you no longer.

Hear no more
your whimpering,
your laughter,
your barking,
your moaning,
your snoring,
your protests…

Teddy Boy.
I remember you fondly.
I've shed bitter tears.
You were human to me.
I am not insane.

You loved me so much.
Protected me dearly,
Companioned me cheerfully,
Delighted me,
Kept me alive
in my dead-end
Makurdi.

Now you are no more.
I took you a puppy
two months old.
I saw you grow
big and lovely.

Promising…
Today at 5 months old
you are gone.

On the eve
Of your death
I travelled to Ife
You were apprehensive
So was I
I was anxious
I wanted to take you
Along with me.

But Death
is stronger than humanity.

Teddy Boy,
on that fateful
Monday night,
December 24th, 9 pm,
you were searching
searching for me.
Now you've gone…

Teddy Boy,
Forgive me.

I should have
protected you better,
insured your safety
at my departure.

Thank you for
your short stay.
You loved me.
I loved you too.

May the God
who created both
humans and animals
decide best
with His omniscient and infinite
mysterious knowledge
See that you go
avenged.

Amen.

Adieu pet.
You'll always live
in my memory.

INSPIRATION

40 ~ THE INSPIRING CALL

First,
It came as a long wish
That turned into an
Uncontrollable desire
The flesh became weak
The wishes were granted
In daydreams

Disappointment was born
Out of this fake
And the spirit being strong

The call was heard clearer
The need was made stronger
And the reality was realised
And the call to take
Paper and pen
To compute art was
Materialised.

41 ~ SOURCE

Adam
I hail you!
Though branded the source
of doom
I hail you!
You, who has inspired me,
To you, I offer continually
A barrel of honey
Two pots of palm wine
Two rubber skinned drums and
A bottle of palm oil.

As you inspire me
You are inspired,
Through my worship.
Your lips would suck honey
To do good things when sweet.
When sour to do bitter things

Of which both would produce my inspired art.
Your palms would pour the palm wine
To soften you, when hard-hearted, and
To get you relaxed.

Your whole being
Would liven to the rhythmic beats
Of the rubber-skinned drums, and
The bottle of palm oil
To regenerate you.

42 ~ REVERBERATING FORM

Best with figure eight
Ringed, straight tunnel,
Beaded by a crown
Supple, succulent full mounds
Softens this form
Habituated downwards
The sacred symbol lies,
Producing forth generations.
Habituated behind the symbols lie
Supple, succulent full mounds
That gives pride and vanity
Resulting in violation of the
Sacred symbol—
Leaving a weaker form.

43 ~ THURSDAY'S DAWN CHILD

I was born on Thursday
They say Thursday's child has far to go
From Heaven, therefore, a long destination
Has been designed for me.
Me, I that was born on Thursday
I have a destination, an end
An end from the beginning
Born on the dawn of Thursday
Dawn that would give rise to days

Dawn is not the end, but a hope
With a beginning. A bright hope.
They say Rome was not built in a day
They say slow and steady win the race
They say Thursday's child has far to go
Me, I will come up big in the end.

44 ~ THE SELECTION

Standing in-between
Two lovers
One as a child
Other as life
Thus, both desirable
One patient
Other impatient
So action!!!
Both would die without me
I would die without them
But,
On second thought…
One has to be more precious
Than the other
Closing my eyes with an open heart
Picked the patient one
Left the other
Thus, having the one providing the other.

45 ~ NON-IDENTICAL TWINS

Sweet memories
Bitter memories
Both gotten
Both not to be forgotten
Set in your innermost thoughts
Yet not to be thought
As conflicting issues

46 ~ LADY EYE

I want all men to court you
I want all men to have you
You who would let men see through you

I want all men to marry you
I want all men to have you as a first
You who would not let them ever thirst

Men through you would see reality
Through you they'll feel their conscience
Their conscience that would let them feel guilt

Who are you?
You who I want for men
Men that would be better through you

I know you
Men know you

You, who men ignore,
Ignore out of sheer loss of willpower
I know you and they know you
You, who is Lady Modesty.

47 ~ 'LA BOUCHE'

In this little world
Peopled with people of
Different sizes and characters,
They are dissimilar—
High and Low

But they are cooperative:
They work together.

Together they share sweet and bitter complications;
Together they fight enemies;

Sometimes it is a world
Of conflicting situations:
Warmth, cold
Pleasure, pain
Good, bad.
But amidst all this,

The constant state of this world
remains cooperative and never divided.
How it were possible
The bigger world
Could imitate
This little world!

48 ~ ORIGINAL ROOTS

Hail Adam!
My Eve, I worship you with.
Inspiration is a two-way
Channelled process
That ensures a
cyclical process.

49 ~ INTEGRATION OPTED

Black…
White…
Yellow…
As you mix
Also share
Equality

50 ~ CONQUERED?

Original CONDITION was born
And lived as a candle
Next came CHANGE
And opted for temporariness
Modernism then came
And advocated permanence

51 ~ BLISSFUL 'PRISON'

No! don't lie.
Yes, it's blissful
Even though prison.
It's a better place
Than your free world.

Accommodation
Feeding
Peace
Freedom
Equality…
Are automatic!

Imprisonment is temporary,
Nine moons only.
Life is precious,
Treasured and nurtured.
A being is appreciated

As a person.
It's a place
To wish eternity.
It's a broken circle
Of bliss.
Releases one too soon
To a vast prison
Of perpetual doom
That releases death
Rather than life.

52 ~ POOR MOTHER

As she wept,
Bitter tears flowed ceaselessly
In massive heavy beads
Down her hallowed bosom.
Now she was helpless
She who had been to many
A concubine
Where were all her lovers?
They had washed on her
Their selfish motives.
Poor Mother!

She wasn't without seeds—
Bastardy seeds
Not one could comfort her now
Now, in her helpless state.
Themselves, they needed comfort
And got such from none

And knew not how to give such.
Seeds of diversity they were
Divided they stood and fell
And could not help her

Poor Mother!
With time, they became fruits, then trees
Through their mother
They saw pity
Sheltered her,
Cleaned her tears
Told her there was hope
This was comfort!!
- To poor Mother

53 ~ ONE THEN TWO

How mysterious!
Infinitum mystery
Pit less deep vault
Blackened with black
Evil becomes sinister
Weak becomes strong
Fear picks courage
Death turns alive
Tormentors oppress
Unyielding, unpitying
Danger lurks around
Canny creatures around
Order of confusion
Need for revolution!
How mysterious!
Infinitum mystery
This order dawns!!

54 ~ AFRICA

Motherly mother,
Mother of a multitude
Sister and friend to a multitude,
Have your children bitten the fingers that fed them?
Have your friends ravished only the good for themselves?
Ever integrating
Ever incorporating
Never discriminating to all and sundry

Though you appear asleep, you are wise!
You are wisdom
Who questions wisdom?
Fools laugh off the ways of the wise
For you are a wise one, amidst a multitude of fools
No wonder you are taken for granted.

55 ~ PIANO

We preach unionism,
We preach we are all one,
All brothers and sisters.

Why do we now operate divisionism?
And also segregationism?
Segregation of black and white.

Let us learn to practice what we preach
Let us learn to accept a combination
Combination of black and white in the same world
Same world that experiences good and evil
Good and evil exist in both colours
Both colours were equal and in love
Made by God, the one God and Father.

56 ~ THE FEET

This is my story,
It is always my story
And again and again it is my story
My story is always an appeal for justice,

We occupy the lowest wrung
At the last level of the body
We look as if we are in the minority
But we are in the majority

Without us the body is immobile
The body cannot be in action
Yet we are never thought of
We are always the last to be considered

When shoes are worn on us
It is to hide and suppress us
Or used to adorn the body

We suffer from corn and aches
Though our stories do not win justice
Our stories win conviction and awareness
Awareness that we're most important
Important for the body's activities

57 ~ ORIENTATION

Are we too big for ourselves?
Why can't we stomach each other?
Do we find this place smaller than others?
Could we be more cooperative?
Or do we try to imitate better situations?

If we can't harbour each other
Why can't we try to emulate others?

The sun operates during the day,
the moon at night.

The sun and rain don't come together
when they feel they are incompatible.

The seasons of the year do not
all come simultaneously.
As much as we show some reasons

in not crying and laughing,
in not walking and running,
in not eating whilst drinking,
in not sitting whilst standing,
let us also try and contain each other
in some reasonable manner.

58 ~ THE WHITE OVER BLACK MAN

The sun was our host,
It was terrible,
We suffered;
The sun deciding to travel,
The moon took over,
It was expectation—
The moon would be our sun
and the moon will remain the moon.

How lucky we thought!
In celebration, we voted 'Iyan'
but potatoes were served!
How disappointed we were.
We got semi-consolation
from expectations of palm wine
but ice cream was served!!

How shocked we were!
The role change contented us
but it mirrored the sun's image.
How frustrated we became!
We decided to be patient;
The inexperienced moon, we thought,
but we were proved wrong.
It's like the host,
the sun, worst.
We are suffering.
We are depressed.
The moon is sun,
and not the moon.
It is terrible!!!

59 ~ THE UNTRODDEN FIELD

A land—fresh and green
Pure and intact
Is the path
Where the farmer, proud and confident
Would invest his rich seeds
To produce forth
Fruits—fresh and supple.

60 ~ EARTH AND PARADISE

Uncontaminated and unaffected
By the ever-contagious fire
Unbiased and unmoved
By the forceful fire torrents.

Still and firm
By the ever-adamant force
Original and conservative
By the ever-communal force

Bustling with life
By the evergreen springs
Untouched and unspoilt
By the fiery hands

What a contrast
To the fiery world

Desecrated and spoilt by the fire
White cladded by the ever-exhaustive force
Now a broken distorted circle!!

61 ~ THE PRIVATE STREAM

A private stream for the dead life
When life is not captured
A flow of bright red movement
Is channelled from an enclosed enclosure
On a delicate passage
The outside world situated
Between two living physical mobile poles
A five-day course sees the
Existence of this movement
When by the sixth
It is dried up,
To revive at the moon's resurfacing.

62 ~ THE SPIRIT AND THE FLOW

A beginning of happiness and hope
To contain existence and produce life
But seeing the Flow unexpectedly
Disappointed the elevated Spirit
A repetition of the Flow's behaviour
Caused the Spirit anxiety and alarm
Another play of the Flow left
A despaired Spirit.

The Spirit tried various ways
To avoid the Flow's reappearance
Only to see it and turn panicky.
In a desperate bid,
The Spirit went from Light to Dark
But still,
The Flow came in,
Causing frustration and crushing the Spirit.

63 ~ THE THREE PRISONS

Firstly
> Is the source that
> Nurtures existence
> Into life.

Next
> Is the source that
> Fosters existence
> Into death.

Finally
> Is the source that
> Shelters existence
> Into eternity.

64 ~ THE NOVICE

Like everybody else
I arrived on the shore;
Soon, I was paddling my own canoe.
At first, the sea was smooth.
Then it became rough.
Soon I was tossed between
Calmness and Roughness.
When it became too rough,
I thought of myself in the wrong profession.
As I wanted to pull out,
Calmness became the order;
It then dawned on me
That like everybody else
I had to make the best
Of both situations.

65 ~ TWO MARKS

Like others,
We knew it was stamped
With two marks.
The stamp to remain
in a cell imprisoned temporarily.
The stamp to remain
in a cell imprisoned permanently.

66 ~ EBBING TIDE

At the rise of tide,
It was green, blue, and gold
An entry into open bloom
But at the fall of the tide,
It became grey, white, and black
An entry into closed gloom.

67 ~ THE CIRCLE OF GREEN

Green,
> bursting with red
> spanned out like a candle
> wax and wick,
> now failing in their duty.

Green,
> bustling with green
> spanned out like lightning
> stable continuity was now
> failing its duty.

Green,
> bustling with white
> spanned out like a second
> time mow failed its duty and
> left green and ash.

68 ~ J.J.C

Green Unmarked Seed

In Paradise
but nine moons only.
Then stamped.
And begins with labour
to hell.

69 ~ FATE

DARKNESS

Sudden dawn!

Panic…

Battle between patience and curiosity…

Lights on forever
Patience!

70 ~ FREEDOM [AFTER AN EXAM]

Tired…
Exhausted…
Spent a mind
Waiting...

From anxiety…
From expectations…
Impatiently
For the dawn of
Freedom

Alas!
It comes with
No ecstasy
No surprise
But with a sense of
Relief

On a
Released mind
That is already
Tortured
Twisted
Tired

But now
Free

As the air

71 ~ THE CYKL

First white
Then red,
A life of green
Candle-like.
Next, a life of grey
spent wisely like time,
then marooned red
and now white.

72 ~ DO YOU KNOW?

Experience is truth
Truth is reality
Reality is life
Life is existence
Existence is appreciation
Appreciation is consciousness
Consciousness is awareness
Awareness is sensitivity
Sensitivity impresses a continuous
Circle of an ever remorseful spirit.

73 ~ THE PLACE OF ART

Should be as a child
Should not be kept
In the bank for
Only the rich

Like the air
Should be free
Reachable, distributed, and
Available to all

Like the river
Must have a source
Be fresh and changeable.
Its purpose not
To brainwash
But to satisfy
Train, feed, and enrich

The poor and needy mind.
Should be in any nature
Of different assortments

For there exists
Different minds of
Different assortments.
Let it live to be applied.

ABOUT THE POET

Olusola Sophia Anyanwu is British Nigerian. She did all her schooling in Nigeria and trained as an English and Literature teacher. She relocated to the UK in 2003 and has continued as an educationist. She is a best-selling author and a poet who has enjoyed reading and writing from childhood. Her father, Chief Augustus Adebayo, was also a famous published author and introduced her to the world of books, encouraging her and her siblings to the culture of enjoying stories. Sophia is a reviewer, encourager and believes in inspiring people through her writing to imbibe the love of God and derive encouragement. Sophia is a member of the Association of Christian Writers, UK TRELLIS Poetry Group [Facebook], Alliance of Independent Authors, Society of Authors and worships at Emmanuel Baptist Church, Thamesmead.

HER WRITING

Sophia's stories and poems are largely influenced by her faith [Poetry from the Heart]. She largely finds space for God through her writing as it portrays faith, peace, love for God and family, forgiveness, repentance, inclusion, diversity and many more. Her writing in in both prose and poetry convey current issues in the world [Chameleon and other poems and Sophia's Covid Poetry]. The Lord Jesus is her inspirer. As a multi genre writer and poet, Sophia is able to find something for everyone through her poetry on every theme in life: romance, fantasy, adventure, religion, family, nature, love, life, pets and a host more. It is her hope that her poetry will create a positive influence on readers inspiring them closer to God, enriching their lives, giving encouragement and blessing every reader.

www.ingramcontent.com/pod-product-compliance
Lightning Source LLC
Chambersburg PA
CBHW051654040426
42446CB00009B/1137